SO-EFN-734

rabtree, Marc.
eet my neighbor, the
aramedic /
2010.
3305227653122
        08/02/13
a

Meet my Neighbor

Meet my neighbor, the paramedic

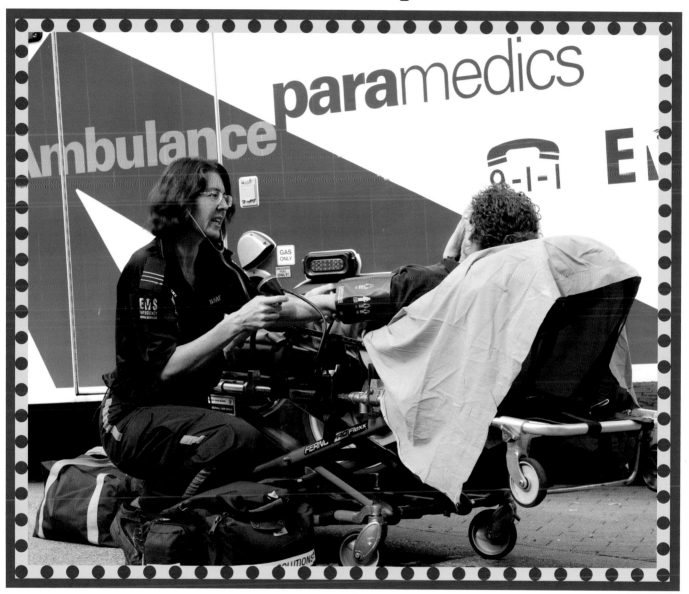

Marc Crabtree

Author and Photographer

🌳 Crabtree Publishing Company

www.crabtreebooks.com

♣ Crabtree Publishing Company

Meet my neighbor, the paramedic

For Roberta and Jesse , with thanks

Author and Photographer
Marc Crabtree

Editor
Reagan Miller

Proofreaders
Corey Long
Crystal Sikkens

Design
Samantha Crabtree

Production coordinator
Margaret Amy Salter

Photographs
All photographs by Marc Crabtree except:
Shutterstock: pages 3, 24 (stethoscope
    and stretcher)

Library and Archives Canada Cataloguing in Publication

Crabtree, Marc
    Meet my neighbor, the paramedic / Marc Crabtree, author and
photographer.

(Meet my neighbor)
ISBN 978-0-7787-4575-4 (bound).--ISBN 978-0-7787-4585-3 (pbk.)

    1. Scott, Roberta, 1962- --Juvenile literature. 2. Emergency medical
technicians--Canada--Biography--Juvenile literature. 3. Emergency medical
services--Juvenile literature. I. Title. II. Series: Crabtree, Marc. Meet my
neighbor.

RA645.7.C3C73 2010   j616.02'5092   C2009-906787-0

Library of Congress Cataloging-in-Publication Data

Crabtree, Marc.
 Meet my neighbor, the paramedic / author and photographer,
Marc Crabtree.
    p. cm. -- (Meet my neighbor)
   ISBN 978-0-7787-4575-4 (reinforced lib. bd.g : alk. paper) --
   ISBN 978-0-7787-4585-3 (pbk. : alk. paper)
 1. Emergency medical technicians--Juvenile literature. I. Title. II. Title:
Paramedic.

   RA645.5.C73 2010
   616.02'5023--dc22

               2009047087

Crabtree Publishing Company

Printed in the USA/122009/CG20091120

www.crabtreebooks.com   1-800-387-7650

Copyright © **2010 CRABTREE PUBLISHING COMPANY**. All rights reserved. No part of this publication may be reproduced, stored in a
retrieval system or be transmitted in any form or by any means, electronic, mechanical, photocopying, recording, or otherwise, without the prior
written permission of Crabtree Publishing Company. In Canada: We acknowledge the financial support of the Government of Canada through the
Book Publishing Industry Development Program (BPIDP) for our publishing activities.

Published in Canada
Crabtree Publishing
616 Welland Ave.
St. Catharines, Ontario
L2M 5V6

Published in the United States
Crabtree Publishing
PMB 59051
350 Fifth Avenue, 59th Floor
New York, New York 10118

Published in the United Kingdom
Crabtree Publishing
Maritime House
Basin Road North, Hove
BN41 1WR

Published in Australia
Crabtree Publishing
386 Mt. Alexander Rd.
Ascot Vale (Melbourne)
VIC 3032

Meet my Neighbor

Contents

Meet my neighbor, Roberta Scott, and her son, Jesse. Roberta is a paramedic.

Roberta feeds Jesse breakfast. She reads him a book before she leaves for work.

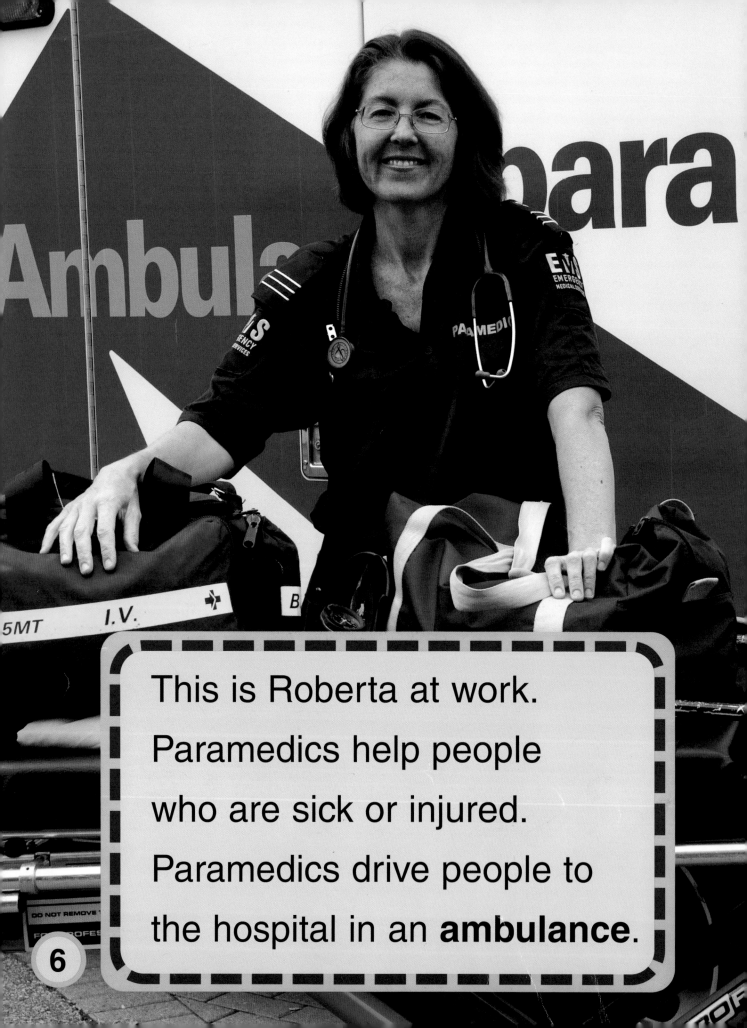

This is Roberta at work.
Paramedics help people
who are sick or injured.
Paramedics drive people to
the hospital in an **ambulance**.

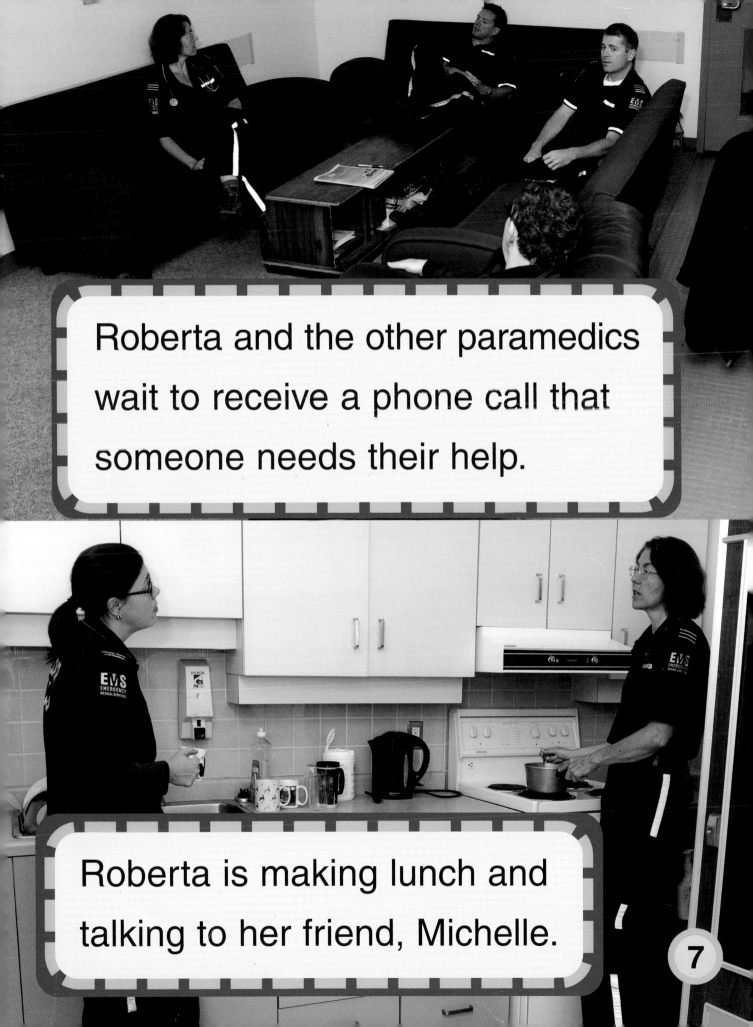

Roberta and the other paramedics wait to receive a phone call that someone needs their help.

Roberta is making lunch and talking to her friend, Michelle.

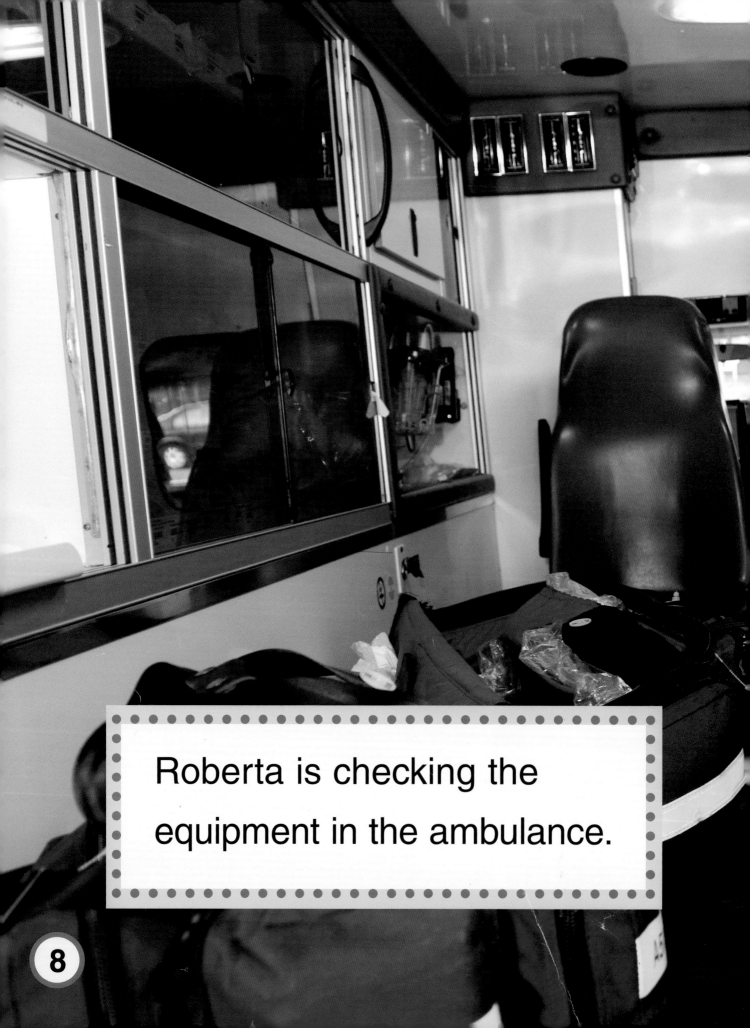

Roberta is checking the equipment in the ambulance.

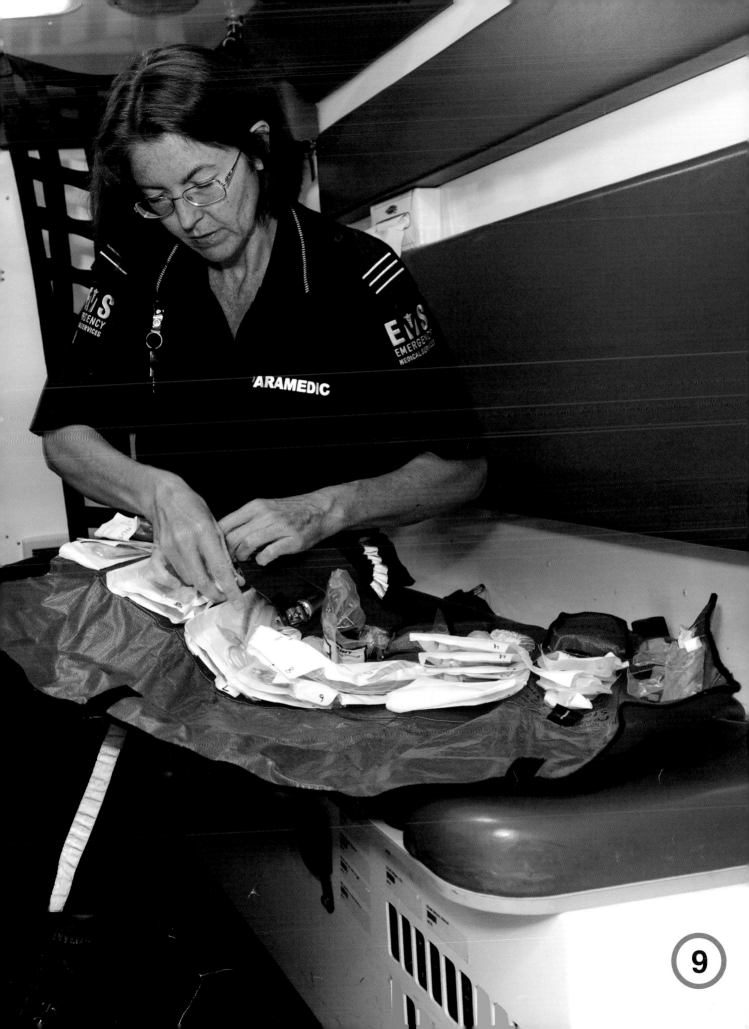

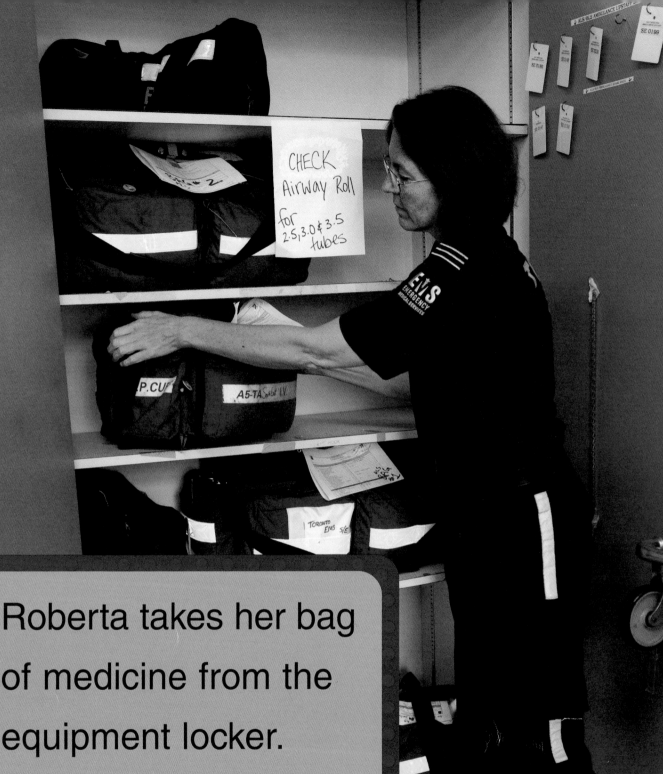

Roberta takes her bag
of medicine from the
equipment locker.
She will put it in
the ambulance.

Roberta rides in this ambulance with her partner, John.

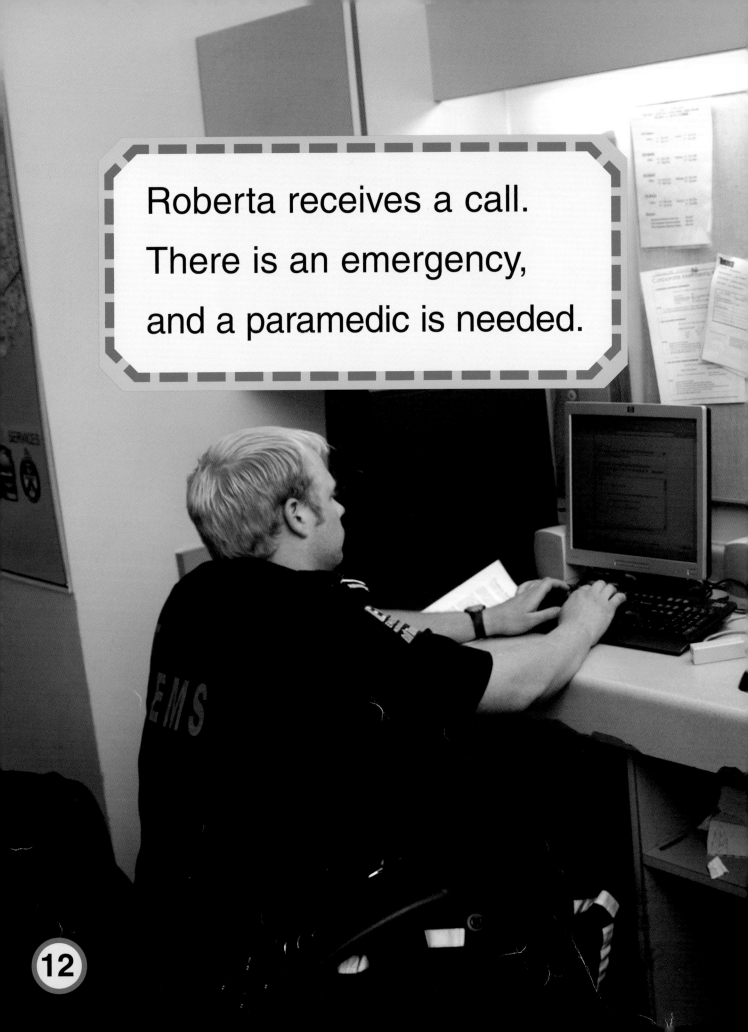

Roberta receives a call.
There is an emergency,
and a paramedic is needed.

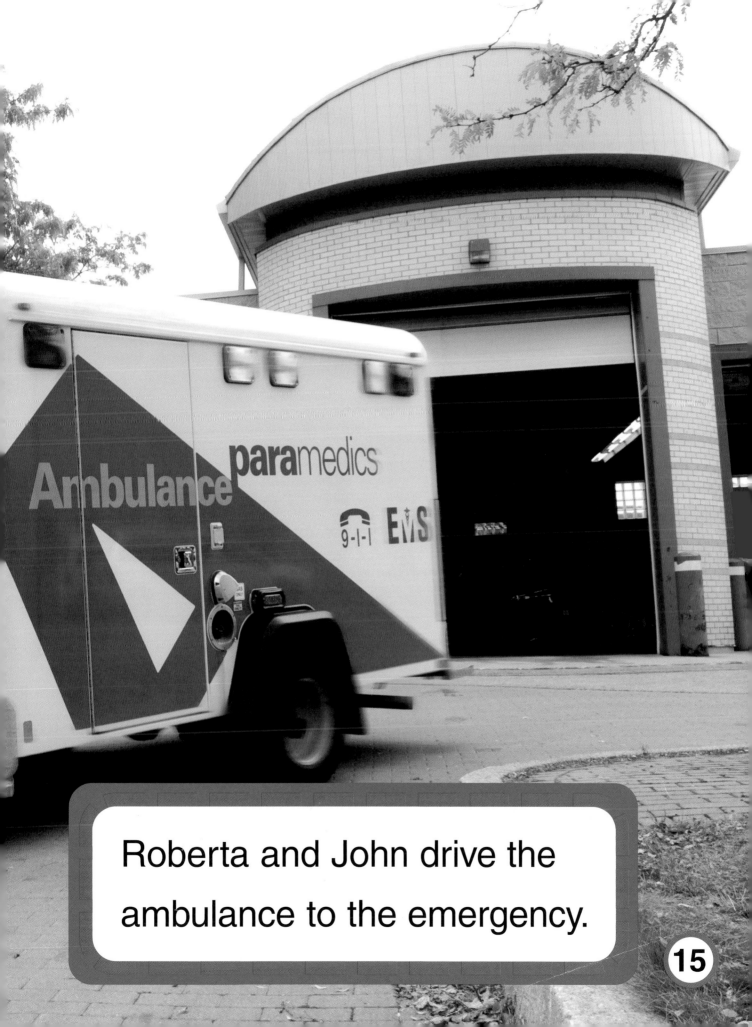

Roberta and John drive the ambulance to the emergency.

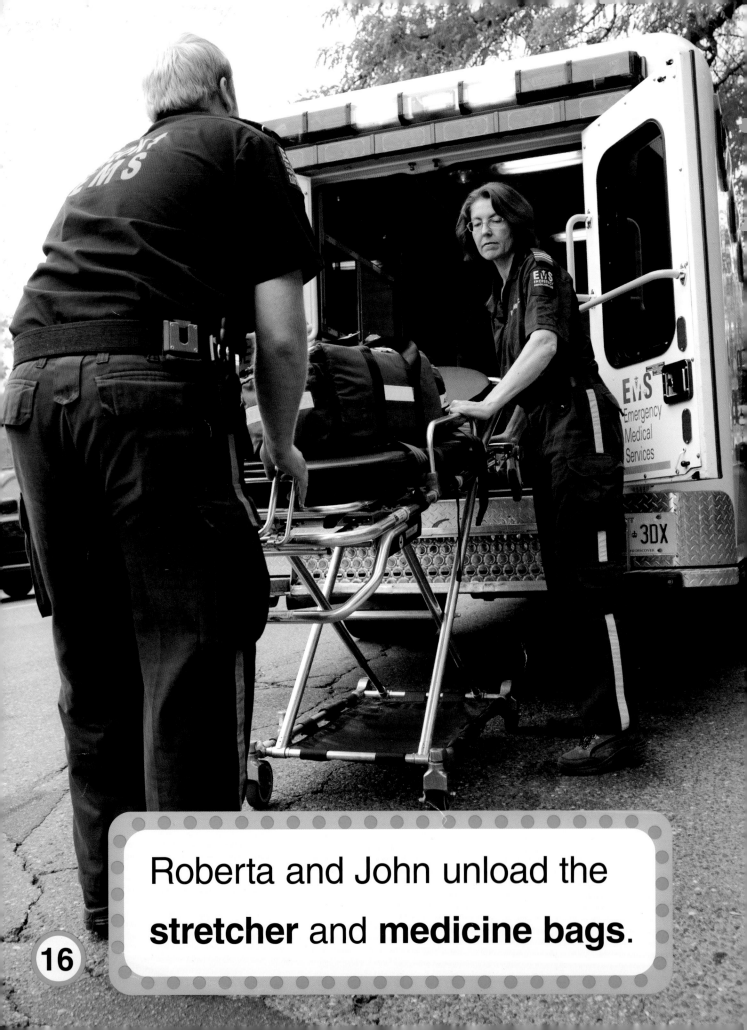

Roberta and John unload the **stretcher** and **medicine bags**.

They will help an injured person, who lives in this building.

They hurry to get inside.

17

Roberta uses her equipment to see how the injured person is feeling. Here, she uses her **stethoscope** to check the patient's blood pressure.

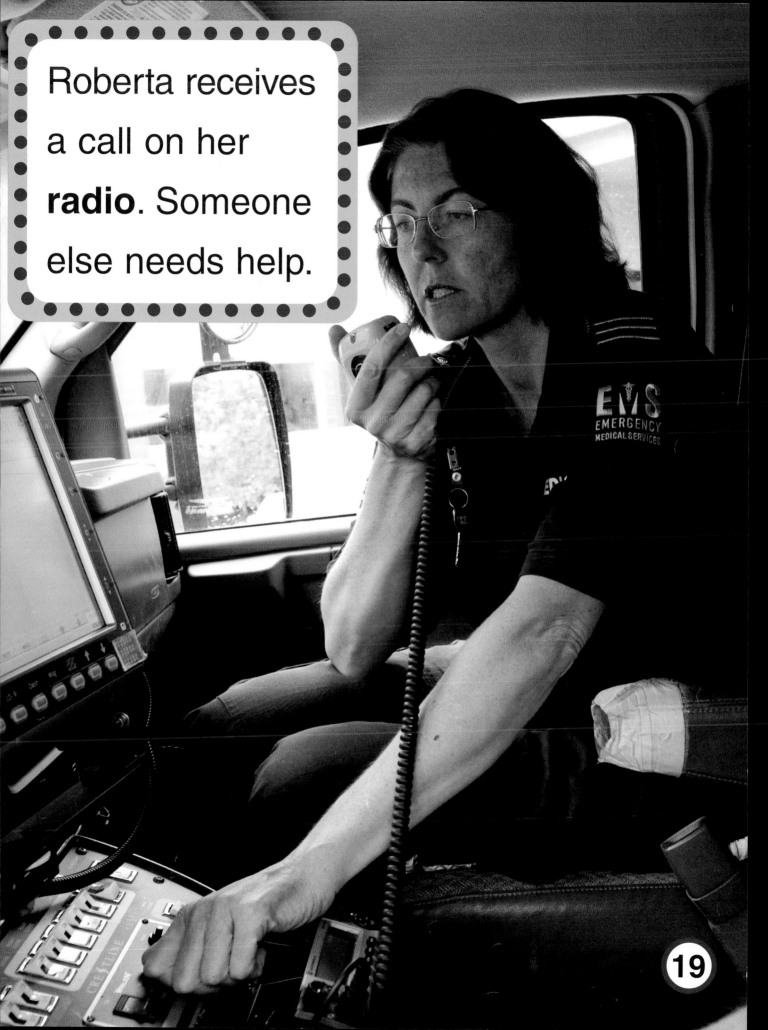

Roberta receives a call on her **radio**. Someone else needs help.

19

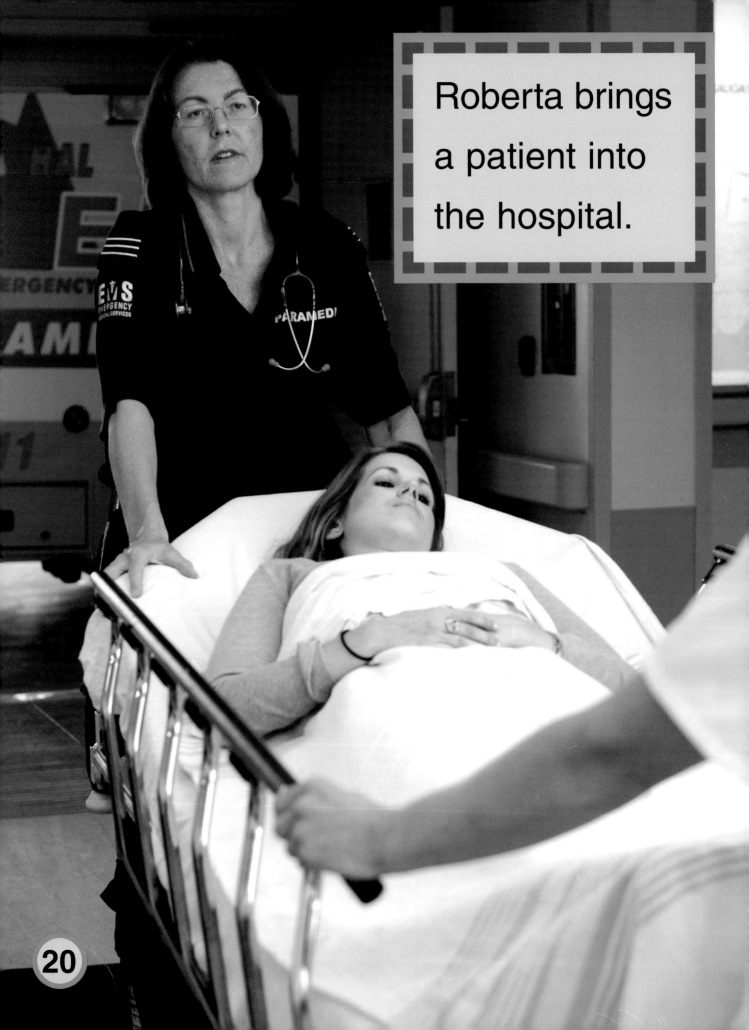

Roberta brings a patient into the hospital.

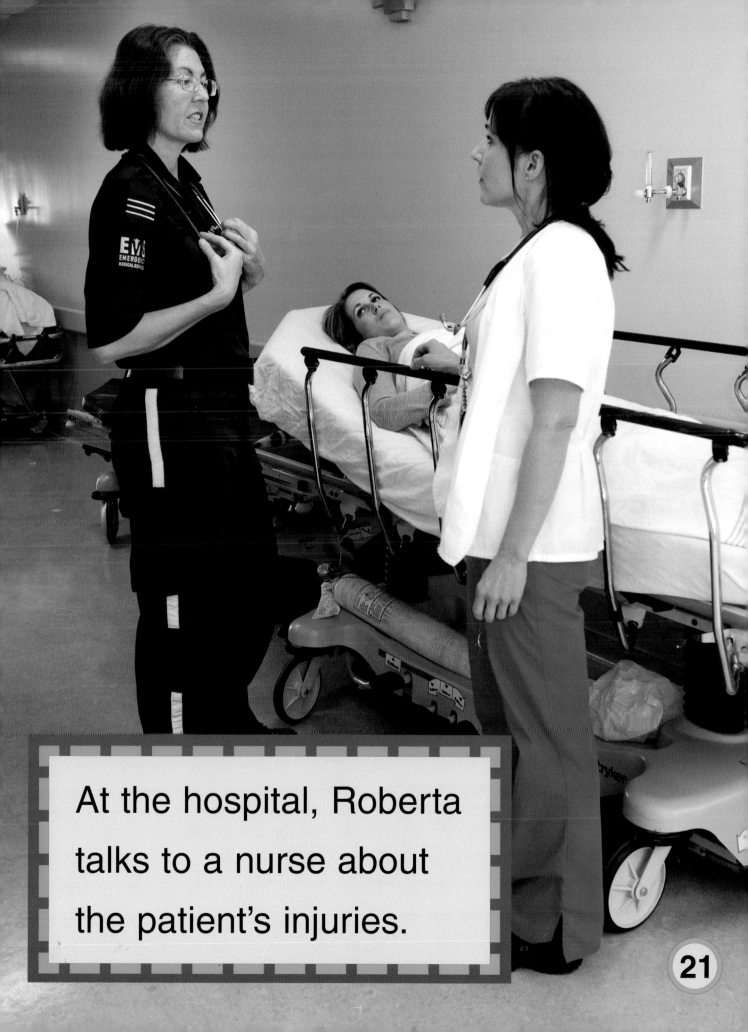

At the hospital, Roberta talks to a nurse about the patient's injuries.

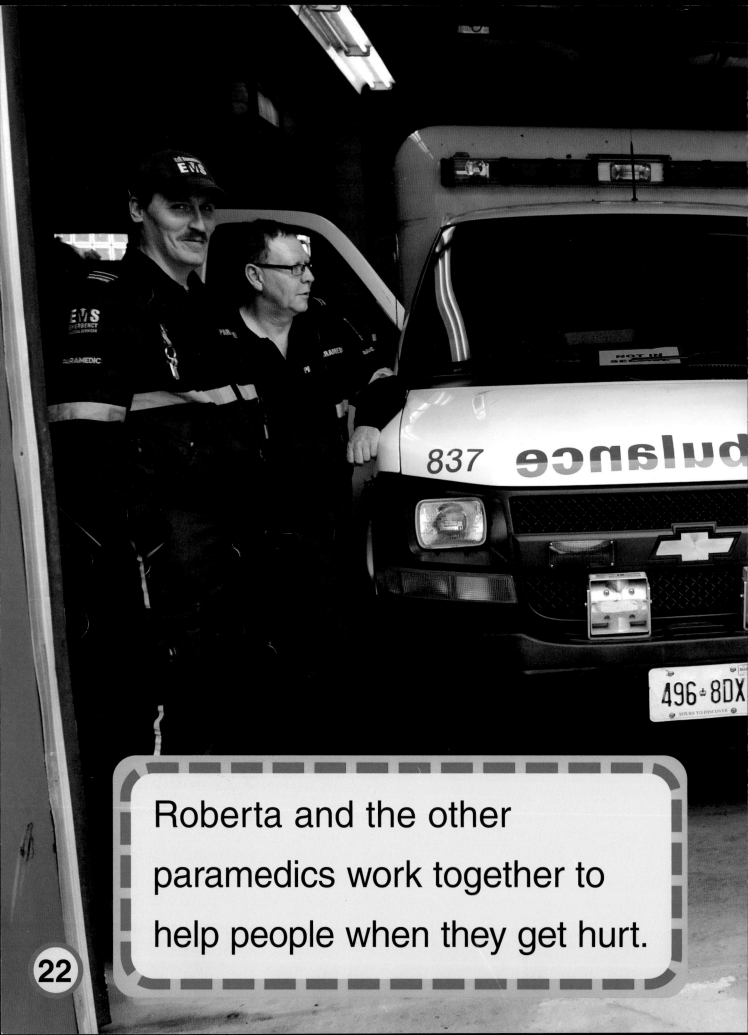

Roberta and the other paramedics work together to help people when they get hurt.

It makes them happy when they do their job well.

Glossary

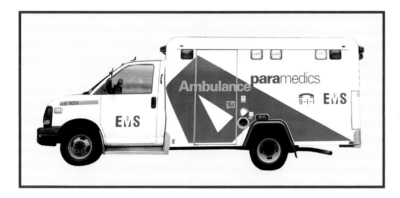

ambulance

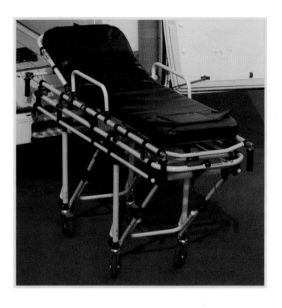

stretcher

medicine bag

radio

radio

stethoscope

Printed in the U.S.A. - CG